PRAISE FOR
NIETZSCHE'S ANGEL FOOD CAKE:

"Oh my God, I love these! More! More! More! This will appeal to foodies and literary types, and will stretch the boundaries of the 'cookoir' genre, for sure." —Erika Penzer Kerekes, Food Columnist, *L. A. Examiner.*

"So brilliantly funny—and insane, obsessive, sprawling, vivid, satisfying, and lush." —Dee LaDuke, Writer, *Girlfriends* and *Designing Women.*

"Absolutely fantastic stuff!" —Binnie Klein, Radio Host, "A Miniature World," WPKN-FM.

"Hilarious, smart, intensely literary, and delicious in every way." —Elissa Bassist, Humor and Women's Literature Editor, *The Rumpus.*

"This is preposterous." —Friedrich Nietzsche.

NIETZSCHE'S ANGEL FOOD CAKE:
AND OTHER RECIPES FOR THE FOR THE INTELLECTUALLY FAMISHED

Written and illustrated by
REBECCA COFFEY

Published by Beck and Branch Publishers, Literary Studio and Micro Press. www.BeckAndBranch.com

All illustrations are by the author except for:

1. The 15th century woodcut accompanying "Geoffrey Chaucer's Stinking Bishop's Tart" is "How Reymont and Melusina were betrothed / And by the bishop were blessed on their bed on the wedlock."

2. Two lightly modified illustrations by British artist John Tenniel (1820-1914) accompany "Lewis Carroll's *Fungi Perfecti*." The illustrations appeared in Carroll's own *Alice's Adventures in Wonderland*.

3. The photo in "Carl Jung's Epiphany Cakes" is an archival photo of Sabina Spielrein.

4. The faint image of the creature in "Mary Wollstonecraft Shelly's Frankenfurters" is the face in Edvard Munch's "The Scream."

ISBN-10: 098540342X
ISBN-13: 978-0-9854034-2-3

ABOUT THE AUTHOR

Rebecca Coffey is a science journalist and humorist. She is the author of three books and contributes to *Scientific American* and *Discover* magazines, as well as to *McSweeney's Internet Tendency* and *The Rumpus*. She blogs for *Psychology Today*. She is a frequent guest on talk shows, and is an on-air commentator for Vermont Public Radio.

"Friedrich Nietzsche's Angel Food Cake" originally appeared in *McSweeney's Internet Tendency*.

"Anaïs Nin's Hot Cross Buns" originally appeared in *The Rumpus*.

"Sigmund Freud's Ten Steps to Great Fish" originally appeared in *Narwhal*.

"Dorothy's Parker House Rolls" originally appeared in *The Smoking Poet*.

"Ayn Rand's Head Cheese" originally appeared in *The Revolving Floor*.

"Carl Jung's Epiphany Cakes" originally appeared in *The Foundling Review*.

"F. Scott Fitzgerald's Pickled Tomatoes" originally appeared in *Monkey Bicycle*.

NIETZSCHE'S ANGEL FOOD CAKE

DEDICATION

To Reta Madsen (1933-2011), who showed her students that there is a fundamental liveliness in any good piece of literature and who had the best laugh ever.

CONTENTS

NIETZSCHE'S ANGEL FOOD CAKE

ACKNOWLEDGMENTS

Mort Milder, Jan Ori, Sally Mattson, Anne Prager, Terri Ziter, Bob Schwartz, Richard Schwartz, Lynn Schultz, Kate Hudson, and Sam Fellows: Thank you for being my first readers. Sue Kochinskas, thanks for the emergency aid. And Mary Bisbee-Beek, thank you for your superb guidance.

NIETZSCHE'S ANGEL FOOD CAKE

FRIEDRICH NIETZSCHE'S
ANGEL FOOD CAKE

DIRECTIONS:

1.　　Allow the angels to reach room temperature. Kill them.

2.　　Kill God. Set Him aside.

3.　　Preheat the oven to 375 degrees.

4.　　Ecstatically whip, as if possessed by a storm-wind of freedom, 1-1/2 cups of excellent egg whites with 1/4 teaspoon salt and 1-1/2 teaspoons cream of tartar. Continue until peaks are as if raised to their own heights and given wings in a fine air, a robust air.

5.　　Gradually add 3/4 cup sugar, about 3 tablespoon at a time.

6.　　You are brilliant.

7.　　Now, add 1 teaspoon vanilla and 1/4 teaspoon almond extract, and then sift together 1-1/4 cups flour and 3/4 cup sugar.

8.　　Blend in God and the angel. Emboldened, add the egg mixture.

9.　　Gaze into the überbatter. The überbatter will gaze into you.

10.   While prancing about in a frenzy of self-satisfaction and anticipation, use a rubber scraper to push the überbatter into an ungreased 10" tube pan, for it is destined to be there.

11.   Bake on a lower rack until done, usually 35-40 minutes, while reciting to the upper rack a long, convoluted anecdote about your childhood.

12.   Invert the tube pan over a bottle for a few hours. Then impetuously rap the pan. Shout, "Aha!" and slide a knife along the pan's insides.

13.   Call what tumbles out a cake if you dare. Call it miraculous even.

14.   Eat it. It is delicate, morbid, lovable, and you will die depressed, delirious, and overweight.

❖

ANAÏS NIN'S
HOT CROSS BUNS

Sumptuous smells fill the kitchen.

The desire for hot cross buns overwhelms.

As does Henry.

INGREDIENTS:

• Butter, eggs, warm milk, sugar, salt, yeast, raisins, currants, cinnamon, allspice, flour, water.

• A 200-year-old stone farmhouse in which every room is painted a different color, and the maid opens the shutters at dawn.

• Restlessness, and just a tad too much money relative to work expended.

• Monotony and boredom. Illuminations and fevers.

• Men.

DIRECTIONS:

1.　　In a small mixing bowl in a kitchen thick with opium smoke, and surrounded by half-awake male admirers absentmindedly fondling themselves, dissolve 2 teaspoons dry yeast in ½ cup warm milk. Stir in 1 tablespoon of butter, 1 egg, 4 teaspoons of sugar and ¼ teaspoon of salt. Set aside while the yeast dissolves.

2.　　Hang a lamp where it will throw Balinese shadow plays on a kitchen chair. Take off your clothes and approach the chair. Don't be nervous; you are in a state of grace, and everyone is half asleep, anyway. In accord with the surrealists, you are about to reach for the marvelous.

3.　　Place one foot on the seat of the chair. Take a lipstick and begin rouging your sex. Everyone has days when they mend socks, weed the peonies, change the typewriter ribbon, and buy stationary. In no way will this be one of yours.

4.　　Combine 3/4 cup of flour, 2 tablespoons of raisins, 2 tablespoons of currants, ¼ teaspoon of cinnamon and a dash of allspice. Add to the yeast mixture and mix well. Stir in enough of the remaining flour to form a soft dough.

5.　　Perhaps it is the utter airlessness of the room, or perhaps it is that you haven't eaten since the opium binge began three days ago. But while applying the lipstick you will come to understand that the sight of the soft dough and the thought of what it could become has reached you in a squashy, pliable place so sequestered inside you that even you never knew it existed. Suddenly tremble. Bleat, "*Eh! Mon Dieu!*" and drop the lipstick, letting it clatter to the floor. The noise will awaken a man named Eduardo, who is haunted by marvelous tales that he cannot tell. He will play the piano incessantly for the remainder of the day. Eduardo is your lover. Or brother. Or is it father?

6.   Demand of Eduardo, "Is the desire for hot cross buns one of those experiences one must live through?"

7.   When Eduardo smiles, release yourself onto a floured surface; knead until smooth and elastic, about 4-6 minutes. Then fling yourself into a greased bowl, turning once to oil yourself on top. Cover yourself with a silken, flowery kimono, and watch Eduardo quickly rise in a warm place until doubled in bulk.

8.   Henry Miller will enter the room. When you first see him you will be appalled by his ugliness. His embrace would be like death, like an orgasm; you know that instinctively. And yet he is so savage. Somehow you long for him to punch your dough down, to say true things to you while he shapes your flesh the way he likes it, needs it, kneads it. The way you want it. Oh.

9.   He has an interesting head.

10.   Any obstacle to accomplishment always lies in oneself.

Don't be shy. Tell Henry how lovely and demure your grey-gold eyes are.

11.   So that he can brag about his bestiality and intoxication.

12.   Which he will do if you let him rise for 30 minutes.

13.   But, Eduardo! You'd nearly forgotten! Read D. H. Lawrence to Eduardo while Henry poses you in odd positions on your belly on a baking sheet.

14.   A Hungarian adventurer will enter the room and ask to use your sharp knife to cut a cross into your buns.

15.   You can only hope.

16.   Beat an egg yolk with 1 tablespoon water; brush over buns, yours or theirs,

17.   Sob for no reason. Feel desperately sorry. Really, it is only out of pity that you do all of this.

18.   Bake at 375 degrees for 13-15 minutes or until golden brown. Or not, if that seems to be taking things into territory that won't seem fun once the opium has worn off.

19.   Don't bother with the icing. Henry will decorate the buns with profanities no cookbook can touch. Have a premonition of great love to come. Become a writer so that you can remind others that these moments exist.

❖

ERNEST HEMINGWAY'S
BATTERED TESTICLES

DIRECTIONS:

1.   In Spain, the balls of fighting bulls are most prized. It's a fine day. Go to the ring.

2.   But make the excitement belong to you! Jump in the ring! Shadow the matador, and keep your head down!

3.   When the bull falls, kneel beside him. Stroke his soft, heaving underbelly. Taking a blade from your pocket, weep from sunburnt eyes, and whisper *"Adios, amigo."*

4.   When using the blade, think puerilely about your own eventual death. Briefly remember your birth.

5.   Stink like fresh bull genitalia as you return to Paris by train. In your cold water flat, and as your infant son sleeps, rinse the blood off the bull's balls. Soak them for an hour in water and lemon juice.

6.   Something about those testicles reminds you of your own literary wound.

7.   Do not worry. That was a long time ago. Since then you have cooked well, and you will find the courage to cook again, in one true burst.

8.   And so with the economy of a transatlantic cable, snatch off the bull's balls' membrane and discard it. You whore.

9.   Now squeeze on more lemon juice, and give the balls a quick dip into boiling water.

10.   Nervous for the first time about the athleticism of your prose, slice the balls into quarter-inch fillets. Do it standing up, man, one-handed! This is why you carry the knife you would use in the company of tramps!

11.   Ha! Take that! And that!

12.   When did you start talking to yourself aloud?

13.   Soon there is bound to be bad weather. Even so, you must find a way to make this recipe come true.

14.   Turn to the egg and flour, for they are words of one syllable. Dip the fillets. Coat them. Feel their gentle touch on your fingers and be happy.

15.   Move on to stale breadcrumbs. Plop those fillets into the dust. Laugh at the poof.

16.   Now! Fry the testicles!

17.   The balls will make a slow, hissing sound. Malice is everywhere.

18.   Those may not be bull testicles at all.

19.   A cow in Spain has committed suicide.

20.   You've had three wives but are still alone.

21.   Urinate. Look at the stars.

22.   That last part was fun, wasn't it? Celebrate. Crash a small plane. "Plane," you must say, "I loved you very much."

23.   Crash another.

24.   You are deeply tired, too tired to eat.

25.   Address a package to the Spanish matador. As an act of apology, put the battered testicles in it. Call out to a small boy on the street, and pay him to take the package to the *bureau de poste*. You, certainly, are in no shape to find it.

26.   Crawl into bed. As your wife tends to your blissfully pre-verbal babe, pull a blanket over your head. Sleep face down on newspaper. Drool enough to make the ink bleed.

❖

REBECCA COFFEY

THE COEN BROTHERS'
CHRISTMAS GOOSE

INGREDIENTS:

- Frances McDormand.

- Bright, crispy, crunchy snow.

DIRECTIONS:

1. I guess that's your bird in the wood chipper.

2. And for what? There's more ta life than Christmas cheer, ya know.

3. Might as well go ahead an' chip tha poor guy an' then pour him inta the biggest pot you've got an' add not ta many peppacorns, not ta much dried thyme, a halfa cuppa cream, not ta much garlic, a liddle salt, an' then more cream an' stuff.

4. Boil alluvit.

5. Serve it on toast, with a sellad an' padayda.

6. And here y'are. It's a beautiful day.

7. [Siren.]

8. Holidays.

❖

MARGARET MEAD'S
COMING OF AGE IN S'MORES

INGREDIENTS:

- Margaret Mead's 1928 observations.
- A modern American boy.
- Honey Maid graham crackers, Jet-Puffed marshmallows, and Hershey Bars.

DIRECTIONS:

1. *In unspoiled Samoa, the life of a day begins at dawn, with villagers drowsily washing themselves in the sea.*

2. In America, day or night, all you need is a campfire. While you're telling your boy to find a roasting stick and stand away from the fire, and while you're reminding him to say "please" and "thank you," you'll hear, MOM? I NEED TO TALK TO YOU ABOUT WHAT WE'RE GOING TO DO ABOUT THIS SITUATION. OKAY? BECAUSE YOU'RE PISSING ME OFF.

3. *After breakfast, girls as young as seven take charge of all the village's babies and toddlers. Older girls spend their days weaving palm husks, or take digging sticks in hand to walk together to the plantation.*

4. Tell your son to place a marshmallow on the end of the stick and roast it until it is goopy. He'll say,

HONESTLY, MOM, WHAT DO YOU THINK YOU'RE ACCOMPLISHING BY TREATING ME LIKE A LITTLE KID? DO YOU THINK THIS IS FOR MY OWN GOOD? WELL, THERE ARE TWO OPTIONS IN THAT CASE. ARE YOU LISTENING? ARE YOU READY TO LEARN SOMETHING?

5.   *Centuries, maybe even millenia ago, the Samoans learned that lime repels the sun's rays from a fisherman's head, and has the cosmetic advantage of turning hair red. Alongside their fathers, uncles, cousins, and brothers, young boys proudly slake their heads, and dream of becoming chiefs.*

6.   Remind your son not to get the melted marshmallow in his hair. He'll say, OPTION ONE, YOU COULD ACCEPT THAT I'M ALREADY GROWN UP. OKAY? ALL BOYS' LIVES ARE DANGEROUS, AND YOU CAN'T STOP THAT DANGER BY NAGGING.

7.   *"Stay out of the sun! Stay out of the sun!" is the universal greeting and reminder for those who spend their day in the village.*

8.   OH, PLEASE, MOM. LISTEN TO SENSE. FOLLOWING OPTION ONE, WHICH I'M TRYING TO EXPLAIN TO YOU, TONIGHT COULD BE A NORMAL NIGHT FOR ME. OPTION TWO IS I

COULD GO INSANE.

9.   *After a late supper, old people and babies go to bed. A crier wanders through the village, announcing that the communal breadfruit pit will be open in the morning. Young boys and girls play with palm leaf balls or hunt crabs by torchlight. Boys and girls who are coming of age escape into the woods or onto the gleaming, curving reef for sexual escapades. The mellow thunder of the reef drowns out any shouts of triumph or murmurs of disappointment.*

10.   OH, RIGHT! LIKE YOU EVEN KNOW HOW IT IS THAT NORMAL BOYS BEHAVE! NO, THAT'S <u>NOT</u> THE WAY THEY BEHAVE.

11.   *When a boy is two or three years past puberty, a friend acts as his ambassador to girls, singing his praises and running messages with fervor and discretion.*

12.   ANYWAY, I DON'T REALLY CARE. OKAY? BECAUSE I'VE GOT A FRIEND WAITING FOR ME. I'M LEAVING. BUT DO WE HAVE ANYTHING TO EAT?

13.   *Girls who are approached by several ambassadors can happily accept more than one lover in a night, continuing in that fashion until, literally and figuratively, the cocks crow.*

14.   ANYTHING <u>REAL</u> TO EAT?

15.   *In Samoa, the word "musu" means adolescent antagonism felt against a member of the family. It is treated as a mysterious, almost unexplainable phenomenon.*

16.   OH, RIGHT. LIKE I WANT S'MORES. BY THE WAY, I AM NEVER TALKING TO YOU AGAIN.

17.   *Musu hurts everyone, because adolescents with musu keep even positive feelings secret.*

18.   OFFICIALLY, AND I MEAN THIS, THIS IS THE LAST CONVERSATION WE WILL EVER HAVE.

19.   *Like western children, Samoan adolescents with musu are especially secretive about matters of love. But there is a critical difference. For example, an antagonistic Western youth, in the spirit of these ultra-modern times, might taunt his mother with, "Of course I love her. But you'll never know how far we went." That might frustrate a worried matron. But a Samoan boy with musu might say, "Of course we made love, but you'll never know <u>how</u> <u>she</u> <u>made</u> <u>me feel</u>." Not being privy to her son's burgeoning joy would devastate a Samoan.*

20.   I AM GOING NOW AND I WILL NOT COME BACK AND YOU WILL NEVER FIND ME. I WILL

FIGHT TO THE DEATH BEFORE I FUCKING LET YOU FIND ME, your son will say. Now he is launched, floating away from you like a proud, red-haired fisherman in his grandfather's open boat. After he leaves, douse the campfire and go into the house. Find his old Boy Scout manual next to the moth-eaten teddy bear and dirty canteen at the back of his bedroom closet. Lovingly fingering the manual, read about how to save a life, throw a rope to a drowning person, drag an unconscious child from a burning building, and stop runaway horses.

❖

GEOFFREY CHAUCER'S
STINKING BISHOP'S TART

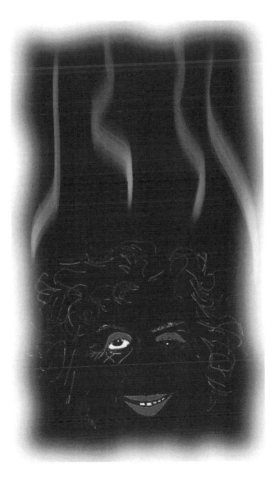

A s ic was cymende up Pippen Hill,
Pippen Hill was dirty.
There ic met a fetid whore
And she dropt me a curtsey.

Said ic, "Oh Whore, ðú stinc so danklye,
Blessings fall upon ðú!
If ic had healf a crown todaeg,
Ic'd spende it gladly on ðú.

"Ic'd wash your nosesthirls, pierce your bloat,
Ic'd dab your froth a foamin'.
Your purplish skin ic'd purge o' gas
And the rotty smell o' urine."

Said she, "Oh, bless ðú, man of God!"
As blowflies lit nearby.
The grasses died where'er she walked.
Would hire skin blister by and by?

The whore she laughed so merrily
And chewed a washed-rind cheese.
Said she, "I've not the plague ðú fear.
I've cheese to make ðú wheeze.

"I've cheese to make ðú gag and moane,
To make ðú itche, to make ðú crye.
It's cheese as foule as rigor mortis.
But it makes a tastye pie."

"It's Stinking Bishop's Cheese, ic see!"
Cried ic, "A nyce and softe one?"
"Aye, from Gloucestershire," said she.
"Come slipe it in my oven."

And so she winked and made a tart
All on a sumorhát's day.
And then that tart she stole my
    heoarte
And purse when first wé lay.

Inside our fullwearm comfye beds
Both cheese and ic were fine.
Cheese pie's in the oven; her fee 'twas
    sumpin'!
And now wé'll súpan some wine, some wine.

And now wé'll súpan some wine.

21

And welle she loofed him,
defite his awfule rhymes.

❖

MARY WOLLSTONECRAFT SHELLEY'S FRANKENFURTERS

In heartfelt thanks to the Lord that all is well, start a simple meatloaf for Easter dinner:

1.   On Maundy Thursday evening, remove 185 pounds of ground chuck from the ice house and place it in a large bowl of cold water. Change the water every half hour through the night and into Good Friday.

2.   It will take all of Friday for the meat to thaw. On Holy Saturday, combine 105 cups of fresh bread crumbs with 55 cups of milk. Sauté 110 onions, 200 carrots, 115 celery ribs, and 440 cloves of garlic in oil. With your bare hands work 55 cups of ketchup, 230 eggs, 220 teaspoons of smoked paprika, the milky breadcrumbs, the sautéed vegetables, and a few dashes of Worcestershire sauce into the meat. Add salt and pepper to taste.

3.   From here on out let every move you make in your kitchen reflect your tendency towards overreach. Animate the ingredients with the Fierce Pleasure of Creation, using your private parts in formative concert with the large implements in your kitchen drawers.

4.   When, in the midnight hour, you pause in your exertions to examine the mess, believe for just a moment that you see in it a bit of hair and eyeball.

5.   Yes! Make it so! Rush to the graveyard and unearth body parts. Returning to the kitchen, add them to the bowl.

6.   Hasten to your library and steal from German ghost stories.

7.   Form the muck into an eight foot bipedal loaf, and place it in the center of a really big baking pan. Decorate the loaf with red pepper, tiling together eyes, nose, mouth, and hair.

8.   Dress the loaf with dill.

9.   Through hours of grey rain pattering dismally against your leaded glass windows, lean over the pan, breathing directly into the loaf's mouth. Ventilate so much that you feel senseless.

10.   Actually fall senseless, letting the early morning Angelus bells awaken you. Look into the pan. By the sun's first light you will see that the loaf will have formed a yellow, translucent skin stretched taught over eight feet of muscle and arteries.

11.   But wait. The globular yellow eyes are watery. And the meat's breath offends; you must have added an *eternity* of garlic. Worse, the loaf is "dressed," yet its coat sleeves are

too short, and its pants are high-water.

12.   Oh, Alchemical Failure! For this you deprived yourself of a good, long sleep and prayer time?

13.   Flee the God-forsaken kitchen. In your haste, forget to latch the kitchen door. Scamper to your chamber bed. Fall prey to nervous fever.

14.   When a few hours later you return depleted and hungry to the kitchen, find the pan empty.

15.   IT. IS. RISEN!

16.   Allow a Cold Dew of Panic to collect on your forehead.

17.   In the time it takes your perspiration to bead, your meatloaf will have learned to speak three languages.

18.   That and it will have developed a desperate desire for someone to hug.

19.   Hear from outside in the square the sound of human bones being crushed.

20.   See the neighbors gather around a fresh corpse.

21.   Notice your meatloaf sneak into an alley.

22.   Call out to it. Lo, though it is awash in freakish terror, when it hears you a smile will wrinkle its cheek. "Mon cher père!" it will snort in roughly your direction, followed by "Yo soy tu Adam!" and "Es frayt mikh dikh tsu kenen. Nu?"

23.   Quickly, step into the square and beckon the meatloaf. Do whatever you can to stop its aimless love-seeking. Offer it safe haven. For heaven's sake, promise it a bride if you must. As it lurches eagerly towards you, blubbering all the while, thrill at the sight of its unhooked emotion. To your humble surprise, respond from your heart with Boundless Paternal Love.

24.   But then catch a whiff of rotted meat.

25.   When the meatloaf pitches itself sloppily to your feet, walk tidily away.

26.   It may bellow and yowl, but grief is Inescapably Part of Existence. Hearing the fuss, the townsfolk will surround, bludgeon, and stab the meatloaf. No need even to pay them.

27.   As soon as everyone has left the square, retrieve your

inanimate animate, dragging it into the ice house to chill for 30 minutes. Cold meat passes through the grinder so easily.

28.   All men Hate the Wretched.

29.   Still, the wretched are Good to Eat. Gently shape the re-ground chuck into roughly 185 foot-long frankenfurters. Grill and serve with potatoes and a festive salad.

❖

JAMES JOYCE'S
SPOTTED DICK

INGREDIENTS:

- Molly Bloom.

DIRECTIONS:

1 Yes O damn you and your Paris fads I am not pleased when you swell me up like an elephant and so no I will not come to you but to a currant pudding that is lumpy like

Lord Byron well maybe well yes Byron had a tinny voice so yes I will come to you and your big red brute of a thing if you must yes please yes appease me yes bring me bread pudding with currants and I will eat it with you

2 Or if instead you bring me flour baking powder salt lemon zest suet sugar c u r r a n t s breadcrumbs egg and milk too I will take my glove off slowly for you and the whole blessed time that you

beseech me to lift my orange petticoat and you keep your hand in your pants pocket I will butter a one and a half pint pudding basin and brush lightly against you

3 Bless us O Lord and the druidy druids while I sift flour baking powder lemon zest and salt into a mixing bowl and

think of Ibsen O God history is a nightmare I am trying to forget it as well as that my slender shapely fingers are reddened with the blood of squished lice

4 Not to put too fine a point on it language is my true love ejaculate (v) ejaculate (n) ejaculation (n) ejaculative (adj) ejaculatory (adj) catawampus ululate piquant

5 Though the streets are paved with consumptive spit your hands and mine together will plunge and rummage the suet then drop it into the bowl and add sugar fruit and bread-crumbs and yes with coarse vigor we will stir the egg and milk into the same bowl

6 Redheaded women buck like goats I know I do Lord I don't stomach the idea of a personal God so before my fine breasts turn to dugs pasty and worn I will turn this mixture into the buttered pudding basin and cover it with greased foil and on the back of my neck I will have your breath redolent of rotten corn juice

7 Everybody gets their own ration of luck and your mouth didn't get much slow music please gents shut your eyes or look at the sea what will the sea care of your offenses or mine and if we steam the pudding for two and a half hours and then let it cool then invert it on a plate you can ejaculate

(v) ejaculate (n) ejaculation (n) ejaculative (adj) ejaculatory (adj) euchre it has a Hellenic ring hasn't it

8 *Deus amo is quoniam is est teres quod dulcis* make rapid crosses in the air and serve with hot custard and with nearly every literary device known to man while you call coarsely to your loved ones dick's on

9 O if only Wilde were alive to taste this and see you kiss me roundly at the Moorish wall.

❖

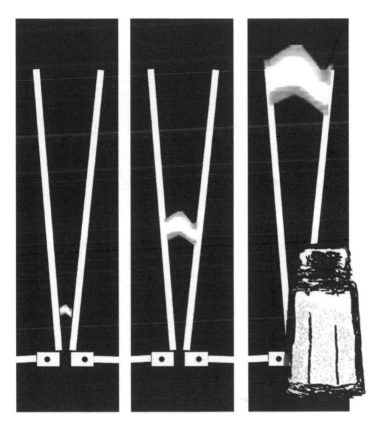

B.F. SKINNER'S
HOW TO SHOCK AND BLANCH
ASPARAGUS

DIRECTIONS:

1.   Informed consent about the intentional infliction of pain is difficult to obtain, especially from a vegetable. Begin your session mildly, perhaps by playfully biting the asparagus. Then ask, ""Did that feel good?" and make careful note of its responses.

2.   Establish a safe word. In an adventuresome kitchen, "no" might not always mean "no." But "David Carradine" (for example) could.

3.   Chop the asparagus into one-inch pieces and discard their fibrous ends. Dip them into simmering salt water.

4.   When 60 seconds are up, dunk them into an ice bath. Their green color will be set. Cooking will stop.

5.   Remember, behavior is always affected by its consequences, and your asparagus need to learn that. If they have complied with the experiment and then not set their color and stopped cooking, spank them.

❖

DOROTHY'S
PARKER HOUSE ROLLS

INGREDIENTS:

- A messy divorce.
- A late spring night in Boston.

DIRECTIONS:

1.   First, let's agree to call them "Pahkah House Rolls," for the Pahkah House is a luxury Boston hotel.

2.   Manners are made up of the trivialities of deportment. Start this recipe off prettily. Check in to the Pahkah House. Rouge your lips and knees, and proceed immediately to the bar...

3.   ...where you'll meet athletic, Back Bay gentlemen singing divine drinking songs and wearing khakis (by which word I don't mean "car keys").

4.   Have a martini. Add another. And another. Do this until you've acquired the taste for them (you've always, actually, preferred Scotch) or until Boston Brahmins become attractive. It's important to become uninhibited enough to put on airs. For tonight you will not be Dorothy Parker, a perennially broke writer and book critic with a tragically sensitive mind, and newly divorced wife of one Eddie

Parker, a nobody. You will be Dorothy Pahkah, a whimsical, wealthy, if somewhat wounded wit of the "Boston Pahkah House family".

5. To do this, you'll need to have yet another drink. Now, quickly, in the manner of someone tucking her own hotel's ash trays into her purse, abscond to your room with three of the Pahkah House bar's best-looking gentlemen patrons.

6. Once in your room, order a few bottles from Room Service. Behave regally toward the waiter. Then pour drinks for everyone.

7. Take the first gentleman eagerly to your bosom. Teach him everything he wasn't taught on the rugby fields at Exeter. Give yourself over to high ecstasies, and make sure to give him a few, too.

8. Repeat as necessary with your other two gentlemen. Pray for strength. Really, put your back into it if you must.

9. Pour more drinks.

10. Mind you, no matter how much alcohol you add to this recipe, sooner or later, you will get tired. Tell the gentlemen to stop. It's only an old wives tale that you should taper off.

11. Sleep.

12. Before you leave for the train to New York the next morning, invite your gentlemen to breakfast with you in the dining room, where the waiters will call you Miss Pahkah, and you'll all be served delicious, trademark Pahkah House rolls, fresh from the oven.

13. As you spread quickly melting butter onto your bread, ask your three gentlemen a riddle: "What is worse than a Pahkah House roll?" Take a bite of the lovely bread. As steam escapes it, smile becomingly.

14. Remember, your gentlemen are fleshy faced, hung-over, sexually spent Bostonians with lovely, quivering souls. They haven't shaved; they haven't even showered. Their sort is prone to mental wanderings anyway, but this morning in particular your three gentlemen will be in no mood for riddles—or for anything from their Miss Pahkah except for breakfast.

15. Regardless of their mental condition, repeat, "What is worse than a Pahkah House roll?" Then, "Really. I won't be offended. We can all enjoy a 'Pahkah House' joke together, can't we?" Then, "Oh, come now." And then, "Ha! As if you three haven't come already." (Wink, wink.)

16. Actually wink and wink.

17. At this point, in a climax of courtliness, one or another of them may mumble, "What?"

18. Say, "Pardon?"

19. The one who mumbled will say, "What is worse than a Pahkah House Roll?"

20. Now they are cooked. Positively braying at all three of them, screech, "Three Pahkah House Rolls! One with you! And one with you! And one with you!"

21. Being Beantowners, at first they won't understand. But with your howls and squawks of laughter, as well as with your pointing finger and the palm of your other hand, which you will slap loudly on the table, you can help them appreciate your urbane, felicitous, noun-to-verb word play. You can help them even as you hand them the hotel and restaurant bills, though the clarity in your message may cloud a bit as your laughter is overtaken by your shuddering and wretching, quivering and convulsing, as specific memories of the previous night begin to emerge from blackout.

22. Your eyes are getting sticky and pink. Dry your nose with the sleeve of the lightweight yellow coat you bought two years ago.

23. There you go getting emotional again. Goodness! It's no wonder men never send you flowers.

❖

EMILY POST'S
CRUDITÉS

CRUDITÉS:

- Looking directly at another person, yet not acknowledging his or her bow.

- An engaged couple in a restaurant, *sans* chaperone.

- A "boneless" hand extended as though it were a spray of seaweed.

- Mussolini

- "Bingo! That's the lingo!"

- The soft bra.

- Bolsheviks.

- Mansions of bastard architecture and indifferently polished brass.

- Butlers with facial hair.

- Hot food that isn't hot.

- Name dropping.

- Zelda Fitzgerald.

- Jukeboxes.

- Australia.

- Pop-up toasters.

- Gloves at table.

- President Taft.

- Dadaism.

- Whispering.

- A parent who goes to bed before the last young man has left the house.

- The moderate trousseau.

- Urinary incontinence.

DIRECTIONS:

Display a select few crudités on a china platter that is hand-painted to depict the slow and difficult scrabble of mankind from the muck of animalism toward the gleaming pedestal of polite social intercourse. Garnish with crunchy vegetables.

❖

IAN FLEMING'S
LEMON CAPER DIP

INGREDIENTS:

- Performative cool.
- Dominant masculinity.

ACTION:

Duck! There are two beautiful girls, one with a scissors and one with a kitchen grater!

Jump! The one with the scissors is hiding behind a dill bush and snipping a few twigs!

Run! The other one is lurking under a lemon tree, shredding rind!

Fuck! … the one with the scissors and dill! Then …

Kill! … the one with the grater and lemon! (As per tradition, one of the two women must go.) Pocketing only the lemon zest, drive to the grocery store for plain, low-fat yogurt and …

Hide! … among the produce!

Ready! Steal some carrots, and chop them into short sticks!

Aim! Rinse and drain your capers! Sweet-talk the girl with the dill into hurling it into a pretty bowl! Add the yogurt, dill and capers!

Stir! You'll both like it on the carrots!

Smoke! Why not? You're in the mood!

* * *

Ranking James Bond capers for quality is a fool's game, but this is the best dip ever. Violent scenes throughout. Some sexuality, language, and cigarettes.

❖

HARPER LEE'S
HOW TO KILL A MOCKINGBIRD

DIRECTIONS:

1.   A person's got to eat to keep her strength up. So Atticus was wrong. It's not a sin to kill a mockingbird that sings for you all day, mocking this bird and that animal, and never even getting into the corncrib or cotton. It's only a sin to hurt it unnecessarily.

2.   Drop the mockingbird into a pan of boiling water. It will shriek piercingly for the few minutes it remains alive, but it's only impersonating a lobster.

3.   That's one talented bird. Skin and de-bone it. Chop its meat, and, in a bowl, mix the meat with tiny bits of celery and onion, also chopped, and some mayonnaise. Be impressed that, even dead, your mockingbird can mock a chicken in just about any salad.

4.   How does it do that? You've got to learn how.

5.   Like Atticus said, to really know a body you have to walk around a while in its skin. Tape the mockingbird's skin to your forehead, letting it hang down over your eyes. Now try walking.

6.   Blindly stumble into the garden. Pluck what feels to be a cabbage leaf and return to the kitchen. Using your fingers, tear it into the "chicken" salad. Add sugar, dry mustard seed, salt, and vinegar. What was once southern cooking is now almost German. Be impressed that, not two

minutes into wearing mockingbird skin, already you can do impressions.

7.   That night, against Atticus's advice, fall asleep with the mockingbird skin dangling across your brow. Dream terribly of the bird's demise—of riotously boiling water, of steep pot walls, and of you holding a slotted spoon and cleaver. What have you done?

8.   The next morning, be so happy to leave the bed that you scoot right up the wisteria tree. *Kee! Kee! Kee!* you'll call, mocking a sunflower bird as you gobble the tree's fruit. Then, mock a bobwhite. *Bob white! Bob white!* Shriek like a blue jay, or, come to think of it, like a songbird immersed in water of a temperature it had never imagined possible.

9.   Feel sad that the mockingbird probably did suffer From deep within your breast discover a rising lament. *Will, poor will, poor will.* Mock the whippoorwill until night falls.

10.   Notice a closed curtain move in Boo Radley's place nearby.

11.   Change *Will, poor will* ... to, *Boo, poor Boo, too afraid to come outside.*

12.   When you get no response, call in other directions, *Tom, poor Tom Robinson, it's our prejudice that killed you,* and, *Walter, poor Walter Cunningham, we called you white trash*

because your family couldn't give you lunch.

13.   Feel satisfied. You've done the dead mockingbird proud.

14.   As the moon rises, climb down the tree and go in for supper.

15.   See Atticus and Jem at the table, chatting cozily about justice and civility under the rosy glow of an incandescent light. The maid Calpurnia is serving a fine supper of fish and collard greens.

16.   Now go ahead; peel that dang skin off your forehead. Discard.

❖

F. SCOTT FITZGERALD'S PICKLED TOMATOES

INGREDIENTS:

- Early evening.
- Casual wear.
- A bender that began at noon the day before.

DIRECTIONS:

1. Having been invited to a garden in Montgomery, Alabama, pick an impossibly young tomato of unutterable beauty. Hold her to your ear and listen to her tell you, in all seriousness, that she is not like other newly ripened fruit. Rather, she has aspirations, and struggles against the nether hell of social expectation for a serious identity.

2. Nod sagely as you listen. Pretend that you care and are rich.

3. Think of her skin flushed, puckering.

4. Actually, for this recipe you'll need more tomatoes than one. So look around. You'll see many. And those sweethearts dangle! Surely, these are the picks of the summer.

5. Silence the first tomato you picked by thoughtlessly dropping her into the pocket of your

summer jacket. Then stride purposefully across the excellently crushable grass. Pick seven more.

6.   Now go home and go directly to bed.

7.   Up early! Work to do! But, ouch. Your head! Have a little hair of the dog, and ask the houseman to bring you more of the same along with poached eggs on toast, coffee, and a quart-sized mason jar. Touch the jar. Touch it again. Make it squeak in a slightly complaining way. Oh, baby!

8.   Tell the houseman to sterilize the jar for 20 minutes.

9.   It's best, really, to wait until noon for your first non-dog-hair drink. That way, you see, the church bells marking mid-day will resonate for you like the tuning fork of the universe. As will those tomatoes. You plucked eight last night, remember? Have the houseman bring 'round the entire bag, and send him away for an hour or two on some pretense of an errand.

10.   Alone with your tomatoes at last, lock the door. Remove your clothes and underwear. Take from the bag the very first tomato you picked last night. Kiss her, thereby wedding your unutterable visions to her perishable plumpness. She might roll a bit on the counter. She might stretch her leaves lazily. Well, whoop! Now you're on the trolley of life!

11.   Grasping the tomato in both hands, feel a strange impulse overtake you. Later you will liken it to the strong, fast, free improvisation of horns riffing hard.

12.   Squeeze the tomato atrociously.

13.   In surprised horror, she will ask your intention. Whereupon you must relax your grip and assure her of your tolerance and honor.

14.   Then, realizing that both your tolerance and honor have limits, squeeze even harder. The growth of intimacy is like that.

15.   Yes! She will burst! So be sure to hold her over the sterilized jar!

16.   Tomatoes lead short, tragic lives.

17.   Breathing heavily, cap the jar and notice that life already feels different, but not necessarily in a good way.

18.   Granted, that tomato was ruined even before you squished her. In the previous night's picking the freshest and best part of her was lost.

19.   Quickly, lest your afternoon begin to feel like one gigantic aftermath, sit at your writing table and describe your romantic relationships in a way that is heartbreaking and poetic. Then have your tea downtown, and take dinner there, too. Amidst this activity, do not forget the other seven tomatoes. That quart jar wants filling.

20.   Late that night when you return to your kitchen, turn the light on and again remove your clothes and underwear. Then repeat steps 11-17 seven times. Neither complain nor falter. Move instead as a boat against the current, borne back ceaselessly into the past but straining

ever more ardently to reach the befogged and surly present. Be like Hemingway. Beat on.

21.   Right around the sixth or seventh occasion of step 17, find it mildly amusing that the tomatoes are of no help to each other in their predicament. They never even ask each others' names.

22.   When the struggle is finally over, add to the jar of tomatoes some well-boiled sugar (2-1/2 cups), salt (not terribly much), and 1/3 cup vinegar along with horseradish, dill, and a few cloves of garlic. Then top off the jar with boiled water. Cap it very tightly this time.

23.   Take a moment to appreciate that both beauty and Hollywood are more compelling when kept at a remove.

24.   As an exercise in irony, cover the jar with a blanket for the remainder of the night. When you awaken, put it in the icebox. You may serve the tomatoes with (or to) anything that glitters.

25.   Oh, damn! Juice, seeds, and sticky sugar water are all over your kitchen floor! You poor son of a bitch.

26.   Ah, leave it. Other people clean up your messes.

❖

JACK KEROUAC'S
DHARMA BUNS

FIRST:

1.   Go, go, go! Nod and bob your head when spoken to. Say, "Yes, oh, yes, *that's* right. I know exactly what you mean." Look like Gene Autrey.

2.   Preheat the oven.

3.   Marry and jump on the couch with a girl with immense ringlets of golden tresses who is dumb as shit and who turns you in to the police on a false trumped up hysterical crazy charge before she whores a few dollars and runs off.

4.   Lam. While on the lam, ask a friend to show you how to write. When your friend tells you that you've got to stick to writing with the energy of a benny addict, say to him, "What I *want* is the realization of *those factors* that *should* depend on Schopenhauer's dichotomy." Really. SAY THAT.

5.   Yes, oh, yes! Get all *in there* with intellectual jargon. Read Nietzsche. Take those bennies!

6.   When your friend tries to write with the energy of which he spoke, say, "Come on man. Those girls won't wait. Make it fast."

7.   The Lincoln Tunnel is phosphorescent on the inside at night, just like you.

8.   Yes, oh, yes again! That's right! Wow. Write it *down,* man, about the Lincoln *Tunnel.* Spit out your visions and twinges of hard joy. No hung-up holy lightning carrying books to the pool hall still hiding from the cops crap. No glad I'm not yet torrentially violent chatter chatter blah blah literary restraint. Dance down the street like a dingledodie!

9.   Grease an 8-inch pan. Even in a parking lot keen minds need things to do.

THEN:

10.   Here is how you park your car. You back up at 40, squeeze into a tight space, change your mind like a rabid animal, circle at 50, *hump*, snap the emergency, and fly out. Wonder if you should make your sticky buns the same way.

11.   Get on a bus that says Chicago.

NEXT:

12.   End up in San Francisco. After a few cold beers become a Buddhist. Let all that dingledodie stuff slide. Sleep outside. Have a rank smell, like the raw body of America itself. Still, look good. The Natural Tailor of Ordinary Joy is your stylist.

13.   Meet Gary Snyder. Go all haiku-y on your wash-lined drowsy doorstepped crying babies in the hot sun neighbors. They work in mills. You have a low, serious voice. Speak in the gentlest possible way to them of sticky buns.

> in my heart flutter
> dreams of sweet crescent roll dough
> hot, baked with walnuts
>
> no lost cause, instead
> sweetened lemon juice with an
> unsalted butter

cinammon good, too.
roll all together on dough
then roll dough up tight

the sky remorseful,
hard-pressed anger and dense cold.
I must bake 'till brown

14.   Jesus, but some mean girl would feel good right
about now. I am eager for real love, saith Ecclesiastes!

AND THEN:

15.   Big trucks roar. Wham. *Innumerable* people, twin
sisters named Babe, tell you the funniest stories, but voices
make you all whoopieish inside. Wonder what "ball that
jack" even means. Notice that your eyes are starting to pop.
Divine that, years from now, you will look unbelievably
bloated on the Steve Allen Show, and Truman Capote will
call you a typist.

16.   For now, though, best not to worry. Dawdle. Think
about Babe. Drop a rose in the Hudson, or is it the Missouri.
Kind of like that it doesn't splash.

17.   Just think of all the places the rose will have reached
by nightfall.

18.   Drizzle with leftover syrup.

❖

LEWIS CARROLL'S
FUNGI PERFECTI

" I know what its that you're thinking now," Tweedledum snarled.

What I was thinking was that I should run. What

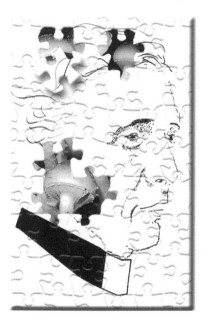

I was thinking was that it looked to be a knife, not just extra belly fat, under Tweedledum's belt, the one with the word "TWEEDLE" embroidered on it. What I was thinking was that I should grab the knife and run to save my life and, yes, that of the quaintly plodding girl with the frizzy hair. I'd convinced her to walk in the woods with me on the pretext of an afternoon of riddles and snacks.

Little Alice knew me as a deacon of her church. Showing her my picnic basket had been enough to gain her trust.

Who Tweedledum was I wasn't quite sure. But, frankly, up until this moment I hadn't cared. Surely my religious garb would convince him to leave Alice and me alone. But when Tweedledum snarled again he said, "And you know what, Deacon Dodge? What you're thinking is not exactly Christian."

How did he know that?

BANG! With a blasting sound, a nearly identical fat man sprang into life from behind Tweedledum. This new roly poly put an arm around his brother. Together they smiled intimidation in my direction. But they hardly appeared to be Alice's heaven-sent saviors. For though they both clearly reviled me, they actually licked their lips at Alice.

Gently as a fawn, Alice said, "Please, sirs, which is the best way out of this wood? I'd like to go home now."

A reptilian laugh arose, slowly and simultaneously, from deep in the throats of each of the blubber butts. Private amusement began to blotch their congenitally abominable complexions. Odd: While their heads rattled laughter, their bodies remained motionless, as though they were awaiting the onset of something spectacular. Actually, I had personal experience with core stillness like that. I, too, could reap a deranged pleasure by remaining utterly calm in anticipation of unusual physical experiences.

But Alice didn't speak that sort of French. As blind to the brutes' intentions as she had been to mine, she crept towards the men to identify the source of their amusement. When she did she spied the "DUM" embroidered on the one's collar and the "DEE" that was on the other's.

"Curiouser and curioser," she said.

Then she looked 'round to inspect the mens' backsides.

It was Tweedledee who broke her reverie: "My dear, if you think we're wax works, you really ought to pay to look."

Tweedledum matched that with an even nastier, "If you think we're alive, you really ought to touch."

Not surprisingly, Alice shrank away from their rudeness. When she did, the two of them let lizard laughs erupt from their throats. I believe it was the peculiarity of that sound that finally ignited the string of epiphanies that I wish I hadn't had to witness upon Alice's appallingly dear face. Childish purity made manifest turned to antipathy and anxiety and then to nausea and horror. As her faith in me and religion and all of mankind were sucked out of her, so were her ideas of her place in the world and of the world's place in God's heart.

Devastated and ever so emotionally diminished, Alice grew smaller by half, then smaller once more. When she finally began to cry, I cried, too. Our tears fell in torrents. Really, it seemed we wept enough tears to sweep us away in a river of salty sorrow.

And so it was that, as if in a dream, I felt my legs wash out from under me. I fancied to hold my breath and return to my mother's womb, to hear and feel the steady beat of Mummy's heart and the pressure against my skin of warm, amniotic fluid. Instead I heard Alice caught in the saddest of struggles. I opened one eye to watch, and saw her pulled by the heinous duo under the river's surface. But I also saw her manage as a stream of bubbles left her mouth to retrieve a small morsel of the *Fungi Perfecti* from our waterlogged, sinking picnic basket. It was the snack with which I had enticed her into the woods. And here is my recipe.

* * *

Fungi Perfecti

DIRECTIONS:

1. *Create a syllogism. For example:*

    - *I hate mushrooms.*
    - *Nobody is delightful who can make a good Fungi Perfecti.*
    - *People who hate mushrooms are delightful.*

2. *From this syllogism, create four simple sentences:*

    - *I = It is I.*
    - *M = It likes mushrooms.*
    - *FP = It can make a good Fungi Perfecti.*
    - *D = It is delightful.*

3. *Distill the four sentences into three implications.*

    - *I —> ~M: "If it is I then it does not like mushrooms."*
    - *FP —> ~D: "If it can make a good Fungi Perfecti then it is not delightful."*
    - *~M —> D: "If it does not like mushrooms then it is delightful."*

4. *Notice that, in the first implication, an arrow points*

from I to ~M, and that, in the third, one points from ~M to D. Which means that already we have arrived at a basic truth: I —> D. "If it is I, then it is delightful." And if I am Charles Dodgson, then I am a charming professor of mathematics and logic at Oxford. More importantly to Alice's family, I am the wonderful Deacon Charles Dodgson. Or:

- *CD = It is the Reverend Charles Dodgson.*
- *A = It likes Alice.*

5.   *Ergo, CD —> I.*

6.   *Now, let us replace the implication FP —> ~D with its contrapositive ~FP —> D or "If it delightful then it cannot make a good Fungi Perfecti," thereby creating from I —> ~M —> FP —> ~D the new implication I —> ~M —> D —> ~FP, which has telescoped right into "I cannot make a good Fungi Perfecti." And I can't. But I can make a powerful one.*

* * *

No, what Alice bit into didn't taste good. But she did chew and swallow it.

A bryllyg sun broke through the dark clouds that had gathered. Rabbits hopped and colorful, soprano flowers sang as the barometric pressure of the day shifted profoundly. With my own two eyes I saw Alice's darling little body whiffle up and out to a size and strength that our two fat farmboys had never anticipated. With Tweedledee and Tweedledum each grasping pathetically to Alice's soggy, red-trimmed apron, she reared back her head, which just so happened to be crowned, like Medea, with a frenzy of snakes.

"EAT ME!" she chortled lustily, and picking her two tormenters off her red trim she flicked them onto the grass. Then, turning to me, she asked with pissileous venom, "Who-o-o-o are you????"

Alice held me between her thumb and index finger like a piece of dried mucous as she galumphed down and up a looping golden trail. As I looked backwards I saw that Tweedledee and Tweedledum were each too hampered by obesity to rise to their feet unaided. They lay amongst the greenery, rubbing each others' uffish bottoms and shaking each other's hands.

* * *

"But it certainly was odd," Alice said afterward to her sister. "And did I tell you that a second bite of *Fungi Perfecti* brought me back to normal size? And that there was a cat that smiled?"

"Yes you did, dear, more than once," her sister said. "Now you run inside and wash up. Today at tea we'll ask Deacon Dodgson for his recipe. Won't that be nice?"

Alice skipped happily inside the door of her grand home, and her sister sat for a while on the garden wall. The late afternoon sun warmed her back, settling a tremble that had arisen when Alice began telling her tale. The long grass rustled, and a white rabbit scampered quietly by. Alice's sister began to doze, and as she did she saw fleeting images of her darling little sister as a grown woman, keeping through all her riper years her simple and loving heart.

❖

SIGMUND FREUD'S TEN STEPS TO GREAT FISH

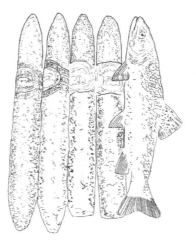

DIRECTIONS:

1.   Buy a dead fish. When the eye stares at you accusingly, think forbidden thoughts. Why not?

2.   Wait until you are alone. Then smear the fish with béchamel sauce.

3.   Béchamel. The very syllables take my breath away.

4.   Cook the fish any way you like, but serve it with bloody beets.

5.   Remove the bones *very* gently.

6.   Lemon makes me pucker. You?

7.   All right. How does this make you feel? When fish cooks, the proteins denature and then coagulate.

8.   There's a delicate balance between perfectly cooked fish and overcooked fish. Does this remind you of anything in your *goyishe* childhood, like perhaps the Christmas morning when you were three and your mother was disappointed to find nothing for her from your father under the tree but mounds of gifts for you, and she cried as she sifted through the balled up pieces of wrapping paper looking for something, anything, but found nothing there? And when you saw her breasts heaving and heaving and heaving some more, you cried, too? And then you ran into your room and looked at yourself naked?

9.   Don't pound the fish. My God, please don't pound the fish. Just touch the fish.

10.   Change your clothes.

❖

JOHN STEINBECK'S CRÊPES OF WRATH

Damn Dust Bowl Crêpes. Start with a sprinkling of milk that gives the egg, flour, salt, and butter just the lift it needs. But your mind is racked with worry about the crops and dying cattle. From this deep unease, forget your batter, if only for a moment. Under the glare of kitchen fluorescents, a second or two is all it will take to turn to your near-liquid batter to granules. Stupid lights. Try to revive the batter with cream, and watch friggin' helplessly as the

cream coalesces into skinny gullies running through powdery, lifeless cinders. Worthless breakfast. Asnine kitchen. Try to freshen the batter with a drizzle of lime juice and pickled jalapeños. Watch the moisture bounce off batter's top, penetrating nothing. Notice that the chilies look like dessicated small game. So typical. Chef Brilliant, that's who you are. Making one last attempt at stirring the batter, accidentally throw chalky ingredients into the air. For heaven's sake. Cook what remains in the bowl. Call it spicy crackers. Wear goggles, if you must, and a handkerchief tied across your nose. Just try not to aspirate anything that might, like, kill you.

How the Heck Will We All Drive to California in One Car? Crêpes. Make a basic batter of flour, eggs, milk, salt, and butter. Brush a crêpe pan lightly with butter, and pour into the pan a thin layer of batter. As the batter starts to brown, gently ladle on dried apricots, radishes, strawberry jam, mung beans, shrimp, smoked salmon, boneless pork shoulders, a naval orange, 1 firm-ripe banana, Grand Marnier, 6 passion fruit, 2 ten-ounce packages of frozen chopped spinach, 1 minced garlic clove, ½ cup freshly grated Parmesan cheese, and your ex-con son wearing a new cheap suit. Season with sensibility, cooperation, and measured matriarchal wisdom, or it's just not going to work.

Ok, What's Up With This Flood Thing? Crêpes. Look. We get it. Times get tough; they have throughout history. But, really, God, don't piss us off. With drought you destroyed our homes and livelihoods. You've brought us to a promised land that is hell on earth. You've driven the men away and made Rose of Sharon birth a stillborn child. Spare. Us. The. Flood. Yes, we can move to high ground and find shelter in an old barn, and even nurse an old man dying of starvation. But no more siphoning excess moisture out of the pan. Give us some coriander-scented greens to absorb it, for crying out loud. Haven't we been through enough?

❖

RORSCHACH'S
BORSCHT

Because liquids
have bilateral symmetry....

DIRECTIONS:

1.   Put beets, carrots, beef chunks, onion, water, and dill on a chopping block and arrange attractively. What you're creating here is a relaxed but controlled atmosphere.

2.   Get out your cleaver and hack everything to bits. Now, did that feel capricious?

3.   Put it all into a pot of boiling water, red wine vinegar, salt, and pepper. Look. You see those chunks of beet that look like penises? What might they be?

4.   And see those carrots that look like penises? What might they be?

5.   What might the beef that looks like penises be?

6.   Did you know that people almost invariably think of beef as male rather than female, especially when it's cut to look like that?

7.   Okay, this is more telling than even I had imagined. Get your stirrer out of the soup. Now. Because I said so.

8.   You'll need sour cream. 'Cause see that white thing there, that dilled and peppered vagina? What might that be?

❖

CARL JUNG'S
EPIPHANY CAKES

Traditionally served for breakfast
on January 6.

INGREDIENTS:

- White flour (or youthful arrogance, whichever is in your pantry).

- Butter.

- Lemon zest. You may substitute a difficulty, as long as you triumph over it by calling forth your Inner Warrior.

- Sugar (or sugar substitute).

- Also: Salt, milk, yeast, water, dried grapes, and 1 "token" such as a bean, silver coin, china figurine, or thimble that you will hide in the cakes for a lucky child to find.

DIRECTIONS:

1.   In a large bowl, mix 6 cups of white flour with ½ teaspoon salt. When I made my very first batch of Epiphany cakes, I was completely out of white flour. Fortunately, I had arrogance. At just 29 years old I was second-in-command at the Burghölzli, a renowned mental hospital in Zurich. That year—it was 1904—a beautiful Russian Jewess traveled to Zurich from Rostov-on-Don in Russia to enroll in medical school. Her name was Sabina Spielrein. She was extraordinarily naïve. Her anxious parents had cosseted her

all her life in a bubble of protection so impenetrable that, at age 19, she was entirely uninformed about sex. By the time she arrived in Zurich, however, nature had taken matters into its own hands, and Sabina's hormonal status had become disturbed. Indeed, she fell spontaneously into waves of orgasm that terrified her, and in the midst of one particularly overwhelming wave, she destroyed her hotel room. The police brought her to my emergency room in handcuffs. My diagnosis: Hysteria. Primary symptom: Orgasms. Secondary symptom: She had lost the ability to speak. Remember, I was only 29 myself. I thought both symptoms were about me.

2.   To the salt and arrogance/white flour, add about ¼ cup sugar or sugar substitute. I told Sabina a sweet lie. I said I would help her

3.   Stir in 2 eggs. Set the mixture aside.

4.   Then, in a smaller bowl, dissolve 1 ounce of yeast in 5 tablespoons of warm water. Add 2 additional tablespoons of sugar, or a few more lies. ("Everything will be fine" and "I will hold anything you say in complete confidence" would both do nicely.) Now set this mixture aside, too.

5.   Sabina spent almost a year in the Burghölzli under

my care, during which time she regained her ability to speak, and I diverted my eyes from her bodice while intoning *Christus, oratorio* to keep my behavior assiduously correct. After her hospital time, she continued as my outpatient. This is when she developed an intractable fantasy that she and I were twins who, having been separated at birth, had unwittingly become incestuous lovers. She believed that, with me, she would conceive a baby who would grow to be the messiah. Let's call this butter.

6. Melt 1 stick of it in a saucepan, and add to it 1-1/2 cups milk.

7. Have I mentioned that the Twelve Days of Christmas are followed by the Epiphany? In an analytic session on that particular feast day, Sabina had a sudden intuitive realization; she wondered aloud whether her fantasy was not a sexual or romantic delusion but a symbolic manifestation of her desire

to become a psychiatrist—and, working at my side, to make a difference in the world. An unfortunate development, that. And, indeed, "lemon" is what I quickly called it. Drawing on my Inner Warrior, I assured her that sometimes even a delusion holds a literal truth; if hers did, she would discount such truth only at great loss to the world. We can always use an extra messiah, I told her. There you have it: "zest."

8.   Pour the lemon zest, the butter and milk mixture, the yeasty sugar water, and the flour/egg/salt/sugar mixture together. What will result is a soft dough, which, for simplicity's sake, I will refer to as Sabina's easily molded personality. Add the dried grapes, distributing them evenly.

9.   Optional: Add cheese.

10.   Tear Sabina's personality apart, forming six or eight discrete dough balls of confusion. Trust, love, purpose, integrity, respect, and even reality would all qualify. Realizing that one of the balls—perhaps the confusion about reality— is the largest of them all, arrange the other balls around it on a greased tray. Think "livestock around a manger" if you need creative direction in the arrangement.

11.   Slyly insert the token into one of the balls. Ouch!

12.   Let Sabina's confusions grow until all of them have at least doubled in bulk. One way to accelerate this would

be to leave her in a warm, draftless room for as long as it takes. More fun would be to engage her in "We're Making a Savior!" whoopie romps for a minimum of three years of analytic sessions, withholding from her for at least some of those years the satisfaction of actual intercourse. (You see, I was married to one of the wealthiest women in Switzerland. Were I to have engaged Sabina in actual intercourse, I would have needed to explain to her about biological reproduction *while putting on a condom*, which might have given even my messiah-focused darling pause.)

13. After the three years, if Sabina's mother lets you know she has received a letter from her daughter disclosing her ecstatic love, sweep the cakes with the yellow of an egg.

14. Bake for about 40-50 minutes at 440 Fahrenheit. Perhaps this is where my own original batch of cakes fell flat. Instead of baking my darling, or even telling her that anything was now amiss, I wrote her a short note letting her know that I was no longer available to be her doctor.

15. Some people create a paper crown to give to the lucky child who finds the token in the cakes. I didn't, because Sabina so clearly was not a lucky child. As things turned out, neither was I.

16. I neglected to respond to Sabina's increasingly desperate letters. She arrived unannounced at my office one

day, and stabbed me with a knife.

17.   Injured, and now the target of my wife's righteous anger, I drifted free of my own emotional and cognitive moorings. Diagnosis: Hysteria. Primary symptom: Everything I wrote.

18.   Set the cakes aside for 3-4 years. This is how long it took me to gain my wife's forgiveness, recover my sanity, and begin my steady ascent toward celebrity psychoanalyst status. By the late 1930s my client list included high-ranking members of the Nazi party.

19.   And the icing on the cakes? In 1942, Sabina died in the Holocaust—but not before becoming a student and adherent of my chief rival, Sigmund Freud, and writing a seminal paper on a possible link between the urges towards sex and death. From this paper both Freud and I borrowed liberally, usually without attribution.

20.   Ambivalent as I was to hear about Sabina's demise,

I found comfort in Epiphany cakes—delicious if you remember to bake them, and full of inspiration!

• Epiphany #1: The most terrifying thing is to accept oneself completely. Well, not for me.

• Epiphany #2: The meeting of two personalities is like the contact of two chemical substances: if there is any reaction, both are transformed.

• Epiphany #3: I am not what happens to me. I choose who I become.

• Epiphany #4: As far as we can discern, the sole purpose of human existence is to kindle a light in the darkness of mere being.

Cheesy, gritty, and yummy! And, heavens be praised, I have so many more!

❖

DANTE'S
BACKYARD BARBECUE

D
They're selling postcards of the anging-hay.
        G   D
That pig's all upside down.
 A7
The backyard's filled with elatives-ray.
G   D
The butcher is in town.

D
That ig-pay he won't hurt too much.
      G   D
They've got him in a trance.
A7
One hand is tied to his back egs-lay.
G   D
The other is covered in ants.

       G
And the uncles they're all estless-ray.
       D
They're sick of phony Latin.
      D   A7
They want a juicy arbecue-bay,
G   D
And they want it in Italian.

D
But hell it is not ancy-fay.
 G   D
Satan's table cloths aren't red.
A7
And God in eaven-hay, in a deep and savage way
G   D
Smokes a better Pork Rib dead.

D
So I'll y-tray to cook in vernacular.
G   D
How d'they say "brown sugar" in Tuscany?
A7
While you're at it look up "osher-kay alt-say,"
G   D
And "ground black pepper" and "pungently."

    G
Oh, abandon all hope ye who enter here,
    D
And ub-ray it on the meat.
    D   A7
Will cannot be quenched against its will.
G   D
Cook it on medium heat.

D
Then give it to Cain and Abel,
G   D
And to ousin-cay Cinderella.
A7
Opheila she's icking-lay spilt sauce on the table.
G   D
Romeo is her fella.

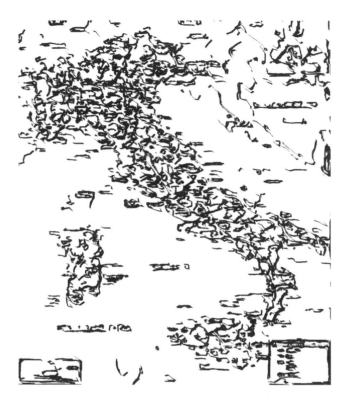

    D
And Romeo, now he's a-oaning-may.
  G   D
"I ate too much," he believes.
A7
Ophelia calls an ambulance-way,
   G   D
And holds him while he heaves.

G
And the only sounds that're eft-lay
D
After the ambulances go
D   A7
Are Cinderella sweeping and me rolling my Rs
G   D
On desolation row.

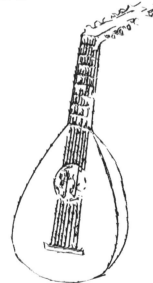

❖

AYN RAND'S
HEAD CHEESE

INGREDIENTS:

- A pig.
- Your body.
- Laughter.
- The occan.
- Your privates.
- Manly clothes.
- Water.

- Salt and silence.
- Onions.
- Celery.
- Parsley.
- Red pepper.
- Recollections.
- Happiness.

DIRECTIONS:

1.   Stand naked at the edge of a granite cliff. Laugh, letting no one know why.

2.   Lean your taut body, oh my godless God, back against the granite. Feel how the spray rising from the roaring ocean far below tickles your orange short hairs. A single thought will take shape in your groin brain: "Head cheese."

3.   A pig will approach. That pig needs you. Lift the pig without effort, and smash its head into granite. Ho ho ho ho ho. One brief moment in battle, and all that.

4.   Now put on your dirty shirt with rolled sleeves and your trousers smeared with stone dust. Bloody them with the pig's heart and skull as you carry them to your kitchen, where you will rip the fat from the insides of the skull and submerge the skull in brine in a large pot. Let the skull sit as you recall your and the pig's brief, shared moment. Then rinse the skull and cover it with fresh water. Happiness is always private.

5.   The kitchen's silence will catch your thoughts and hold them. This is when you should add the pig's heart to the pot and set everything to boil.

6.   Oh, blessed be the tie that binds! Now! Go! Chop the pig's heart!

7. You are handsome like a law of nature, and no one can quite name why.

8. Onions, celery, parsley, and red pepper must all sacrifice their vegetable existences. Chop them, add them, and, in an uncharacteristic gesture of tenderness, as the brew boils think with curiosity of the pig. Always the pig. The meat will separate from the skull.

9. Strain away the water so that you can shape what remains and refrigerate it. But do not look at it, except with contempt. That should drive it wild.

10. Remember the cliff. Remember the rocks holding you firmly.

11. In the kitchen, step as if to the edge of the cliff. Don't be shy. Raise your arms as if to dive, or in salute to the sacrifices you require of others. This moment is like a point reached, a stop in the movement of your life.

12. And you look Olympian.

13. But fat lot of good that will do you with the authorities.

14. The days ahead will be difficult, with questions to face. Accept that if you kill the pig alone, you eat head cheese that way, too.

❖

NIETZSCHE'S ANGEL FOOD CAKE

Look for Rebecca Coffey's serio-comic novel,
HYSTERICAL: Anna Freud's Story,
to be published in the spring of 2014.

NIETZSCHE'S ANGEL FOOD CAKE